This Business Journal Belongs To:

_____

Suppliers LIST

PRODUCT:	DESCRIPTION:	COMPANY/VENDOR:	WEBSITE URL:

Supply INVENTORY

PRODUCT:	SUPPLIER:	QTY:	COST:

Monthly SALES

DATE:	SOURCE	PRICE:	PROFIT:

Monthly INCOME TRACKER

MONTH: _____   **YEAR:** _____

DATE:	DESCRIPTION:	GROSS:	NET:

Monthly EXPENSES

MONTH: **YEAR:**

DATE:	DESCRIPTION:	INVOICE #:	AMOUNT:

Monthly BUDGET

MONTH: _____   **YEAR:** _____

OVERVIEW:	BUDGETED:	ACTUAL COST:
INCOME:		
EXPENSES:		
SAVINGS:		
OTHER:		

EXPENSE TRACKER

SUMMARY:	BUDGETED:	ACTUAL COST:	NOTES:

Product INVENTORY

PRODUCT:	DESCRIPTION:	QTY:	COST:

Mileage TRACKER

PERIOD OF: _____

DATE:	TO:	FROM:	PURPOSE:	TOTAL DISTANCE

Product PRICING

ITEM:	SUPPLY COST:	LABOR:	SHIPPING COST:	PROFIT:

Tax DEDUCTIONS

MONTH: _____   **YEAR:** _____

DATE:	DESCRIPTION:	AMOUNT:	NOTES:

Discount TRACKER

MONTH: **YEAR:**

ITEM:	DESCRIPTION:	REG PRICE:	SALE PRICE:

$Shipping$ TRACKER

ORDER #:	PRODUCT DESCRIPTION:	SHIP DATE:	TRACKING #:	SHIPPED:

Supplier CONTACTS

NAME	NAME
BUSINESS	BUSINESS
WEBSITE:	WEBSITE:
EMAIL:	EMAIL:
PHONE:	PHONE:

BUSINESS	BUSINESS
WEBSITE:	WEBSITE:
EMAIL:	EMAIL:
PHONE:	PHONE:

BUSINESS	BUSINESS
WEBSITE:	WEBSITE:
EMAIL:	EMAIL:
PHONE:	PHONE:

BUSINESS	BUSINESS
WEBSITE:	WEBSITE:
EMAIL:	EMAIL:
PHONE:	PHONE:

BUSINESS	BUSINESS
WEBSITE:	WEBSITE:
EMAIL:	EMAIL:
PHONE:	PHONE:

Shipping TRACKER

ORDER NUMBER:	DESCRIPTION OF ITEM:	SHIP DATE:	TRACKING #:

Returns TRACKER

ORDER DATE:	ORDER #:	ITEM DESCRIPTION:	REASON:

Monthly SALES

JANUARY

FEBRUARY

MARCH

APRIL

MAY

JUNE

Monthly SALES

JULY

AUGUST

SEPTEMBER

OCTOBER

NOVEMBER

DECEMBER

Product PLANNER

PRODUCT DESCRIPTION:

SUPPLIES NEEDED:

PRODUCTION COST BREAKDOWN & EXPENSES

SUPPLIES:

MATERIALS:

LABOR:

SHIPPING:

FEES:

OTHER:

STORAGE:

TOTAL COST:

IMPORTANT NOTES

OTHER INFORMATION

Marketing PLANNER

MONTH: ....

RESOURCES:

START: _____ **END:** _____

ADVERTISING BREAKDOWN & OVERVIEW

CAMPAIGN: _____ **BUDGET:** _____

AUDIENCE: _____ **COST:** _____

REACH: _____ **LEADS:** _____

TRAFFIC: _____ **REBOOK:** _____

IMPORTANT NOTES

Monthly BUSINESS GOALS

YEAR: ....

JANUARY	FEBRUARY	MARCH

APRIL	MAY	JUNE

JULY	AUGUST	SEPTEMBER

OCTOBER	NOVEMBER	DECEMBER

NOTES:

Yearly BUSINESS GOALS

YEAR:

MAIN OBJECTIVE:

GOAL #1:	GOAL #2:

STEPS I'LL TAKE TO ACHIEVE MY GOALS:

GOAL THIS WILL ACCOMPLISH

Notes

$\mathcal{My}$ BUSINESS GOALS

GOAL

START DATE: DATE OF COMPLETION:

GOAL PROGRESS

GOAL

START DATE: DATE OF COMPLETION:

GOAL PROGRESS

GOAL

START DATE: DATE OF COMPLETION:

GOAL PROGRESS

GOAL

START DATE: DATE OF COMPLETION:

GOAL PROGRESS

GOAL

START DATE: DATE OF COMPLETION:

GOAL PROGRESS

GOAL

START DATE: DATE OF COMPLETION::

GOAL PROGRESS

IMPORTANT NOTES	**REMINDERS**

My BUSINESS GOALS

GOAL

PRIORITY:

🕐 START DATE: DEADLINE:

STEPS TO ACHIEVE MY GOAL:

ACTION STEPS	COMPLETE BY	NOTES

MILESTONES   MILESTONES   MILESTONES

Order FORM

DATE		ORDER #:

CUSTOMER:	EMAIL:	PHONE #:

MAILING ADDRESS:

ITEM#	DESCRIPTION	QTY	PRICE	CUSTOMER NOTES

 # OF PRODUCTS ORDERED:

TOTAL UNIT PRICE: TAX:

APPLIED DISCOUNTS: SHIPPING COST:

PAYMENT METHOD: ORDER DATE:

TOTAL COST:

Order TRACKER

DATE | ORDER #:

CUSTOMER: | EMAIL: | PHONE #:

PRODUCT:	QTY	SHIP DATE		PRODUCT:	QTY	SHIP DATE
			☐				☐
			☐				☐
			☐				☐
			☐				☐
			☐				☐
			☐				☐

TRACKING NUMBER: | DELIVERED

NOTES:

DATE | ORDER #:

CUSTOMER: | EMAIL: | PHONE #:

PRODUCT:	QTY	SHIP DATE		PRODUCT:	QTY	SHIP DATE
			☐				☐
			☐				☐
			☐				☐
			☐				☐
			☐				☐
			☐				☐

TRACKING NUMBER: | DELIVERED

NOTES:

Weekly BUSINESS GOALS

WEEK OF: ....

GOAL:

- [ ] _____
- [ ] _____
- [ ] _____
- [ ] _____
- [ ] _____
- [ ] _____
- [ ] _____

GOAL:

- [ ] _____
- [ ] _____
- [ ] _____
- [ ] _____
- [ ] _____
- [ ] _____
- [ ] _____

GOAL:

- [ ] _____
- [ ] _____
- [ ] _____
- [ ] _____
- [ ] _____
- [ ] _____
- [ ] _____

GOAL:

- [ ] _____
- [ ] _____
- [ ] _____
- [ ] _____
- [ ] _____
- [ ] _____

GOAL:

- [ ] _____
- [ ] _____
- [ ] _____
- [ ] _____
- [ ] _____
- [ ] _____
- [ ] _____

GOAL:

- [ ] _____
- [ ] _____
- [ ] _____
- [ ] _____
- [ ] _____
- [ ] _____

Business NOTES

Ideas

Notes

Monthly SALES

DATE:	SOURCE	PRICE:	PROFIT:

Monthly INCOME TRACKER

MONTH: **YEAR:**

DATE:	DESCRIPTION:	GROSS:	NET:

Monthly EXPENSES

MONTH: _____   **YEAR:** _____

DATE:	DESCRIPTION:	INVOICE #:	AMOUNT:

Monthly BUDGET

MONTH: ....   **YEAR:** ....

OVERVIEW:	BUDGETED:	ACTUAL COST:
INCOME:		
EXPENSES:		
SAVINGS:		
OTHER:		

EXPENSE TRACKER

SUMMARY:	BUDGETED:	ACTUAL COST:	NOTES:

Product INVENTORY

PRODUCT:	DESCRIPTION:	QTY:	COST:

Mileage TRACKER

PERIOD OF:

DATE:	TO:	FROM:	PURPOSE:	TOTAL DISTANCE

Product PRICING

ITEM:	SUPPLY COST:	LABOR:	SHIPPING COST:	PROFIT:

Tax DEDUCTIONS

MONTH: **YEAR:**

DATE:	DESCRIPTION:	AMOUNT:	NOTES:

Discount TRACKER

MONTH: _____   **YEAR:** _____

ITEM:	DESCRIPTION:	REG PRICE:	SALE PRICE:

Shipping TRACKER

ORDER #:	PRODUCT DESCRIPTION:	SHIP DATE:	TRACKING #:	SHIPPED:

Supplier CONTACTS

NAME	NAME
BUSINESS	BUSINESS
WEBSITE:	WEBSITE:
EMAIL:	EMAIL:
PHONE:	PHONE:

BUSINESS	BUSINESS
WEBSITE:	WEBSITE:
EMAIL:	EMAIL:
PHONE:	PHONE:

BUSINESS	BUSINESS
WEBSITE:	WEBSITE:
EMAIL:	EMAIL:
PHONE:	PHONE:

BUSINESS	BUSINESS
WEBSITE:	WEBSITE:
EMAIL:	EMAIL:
PHONE:	PHONE:

BUSINESS	BUSINESS
WEBSITE:	WEBSITE:
EMAIL:	EMAIL:
PHONE:	PHONE:

Shipping TRACKER

ORDER NUMBER:	DESCRIPTION OF ITEM:	SHIP DATE:	TRACKING #:

Returns TRACKER

ORDER DATE:	ORDER #:	ITEM DESCRIPTION:	REASON:

Monthly SALES

JANUARY

FEBRUARY

MARCH

APRIL

MAY

JUNE

Monthly SALES

JULY	AUGUST	SEPTEMBER

OCTOBER	NOVEMBER	DECEMBER

Product PLANNER

PRODUCT DESCRIPTION:

SUPPLIES NEEDED:

PRODUCTION COST BREAKDOWN & EXPENSES

SUPPLIES:

MATERIALS:

LABOR:

SHIPPING:

FEES:

OTHER:

STORAGE:

TOTAL COST:

IMPORTANT NOTES

OTHER INFORMATION

Marketing PLANNER

MONTH: ....

RESOURCES:

START: _____ **END:** _____

ADVERTISING BREAKDOWN & OVERVIEW

CAMPAIGN: _____

BUDGET: _____

AUDIENCE: _____

COST: _____

REACH: _____

LEADS: _____

TRAFFIC: _____

REBOOK: _____

IMPORTANT NOTES

Monthly BUSINESS GOALS

YEAR: ....

JANUARY	FEBRUARY	MARCH

APRIL	MAY	JUNE

JULY	AUGUST	SEPTEMBER

OCTOBER	NOVEMBER	DECEMBER

NOTES:

Yearly BUSINESS GOALS

YEAR:

MAIN OBJECTIVE:

GOAL #1:

GOAL #2:

STEPS I'LL TAKE TO ACHIEVE MY GOALS:

GOAL THIS WILL ACCOMPLISH

Notes

My BUSINESS GOALS

GOAL

START DATE: DATE OF COMPLETION:

GOAL PROGRESS

GOAL

START DATE: DATE OF COMPLETION:

GOAL PROGRESS

GOAL

START DATE: DATE OF COMPLETION:

GOAL PROGRESS

GOAL

START DATE: DATE OF COMPLETION:

GOAL PROGRESS

GOAL

START DATE: DATE OF COMPLETION:

GOAL PROGRESS

GOAL

START DATE: DATE OF COMPLETION::

GOAL PROGRESS

IMPORTANT NOTES	REMINDERS

My BUSINESS GOALS

GOAL

PRIORITY:

🕐 START DATE: DEADLINE:

STEPS TO ACHIEVE MY GOAL:

ACTION STEPS	COMPLETE BY	NOTES

MILESTONES	MILESTONES	MILESTONES

Order FORM

DATE		ORDER #:

CUSTOMER:	EMAIL:	PHONE #:

MAILING ADDRESS:

ITEM#	DESCRIPTION	QTY	PRICE	CUSTOMER NOTES

 # OF PRODUCTS ORDERED:

TOTAL UNIT PRICE: TAX:

APPLIED DISCOUNTS: SHIPPING COST:

PAYMENT METHOD: ORDER DATE:

TOTAL COST:

Order TRACKER

DATE | | ORDER #:

CUSTOMER: | EMAIL: | PHONE #:

PRODUCT:	QTY	SHIP DATE		PRODUCT:	QTY	SHIP DATE
		☐				☐
		☐				☐
		☐				☐
		☐				☐
		☐				☐
		☐				☐

TRACKING NUMBER: | DELIVERED

NOTES:

DATE | | ORDER #:

CUSTOMER: | EMAIL: | PHONE #:

PRODUCT:	QTY	SHIP DATE		PRODUCT:	QTY	SHIP DATE
		☐				☐
		☐				☐
		☐				☐
		☐				☐
		☐				☐
		☐				☐

TRACKING NUMBER: | DELIVERED

NOTES:

Weekly BUSINESS GOALS

WEEK OF: ....

GOAL:

- [ ] ....
- [ ] ....
- [ ] ....
- [ ] ....
- [ ] ....
- [ ] ....
- [ ] ....

GOAL:

- [ ] ....
- [ ] ....
- [ ] ....
- [ ] ....
- [ ] ....
- [ ] ....
- [ ] ....

GOAL:

- [ ] ....
- [ ] ....
- [ ] ....
- [ ] ....
- [ ] ....
- [ ] ....
- [ ] ....

GOAL:

- [ ] ....
- [ ] ....
- [ ] ....
- [ ] ....
- [ ] ....
- [ ] ....

GOAL:

- [ ] ....
- [ ] ....
- [ ] ....
- [ ] ....
- [ ] ....
- [ ] ....

GOAL:

- [ ] ....
- [ ] ....
- [ ] ....
- [ ] ....
- [ ] ....
- [ ] ....

Business NOTES

_____

_____

_____

_____

_____

_____

_____

_____

_____

_____

_____

_____

_____

_____

_____

_____

_____

Ideas	*Notes*

Monthly SALES

DATE:	SOURCE	PRICE:	PROFIT:

Monthly INCOME TRACKER

MONTH: _____   **YEAR:** _____

DATE:	DESCRIPTION:	GROSS:	NET:

Monthly EXPENSES

MONTH: **YEAR:**

DATE:	DESCRIPTION:	INVOICE #:	AMOUNT:

Monthly BUDGET

MONTH: _____   **YEAR:** _____

OVERVIEW:	BUDGETED:	ACTUAL COST:
INCOME:		
EXPENSES:		
SAVINGS:		
OTHER:		

EXPENSE TRACKER

SUMMARY:	BUDGETED:	ACTUAL COST	NOTES:

Product INVENTORY

PRODUCT:	DESCRIPTION:	QTY:	COST:

Mileage TRACKER

PERIOD OF: _____

DATE:	TO:	FROM:	PURPOSE:	TOTAL DISTANCE

Product PRICING

ITEM:	SUPPLY COST:	LABOR:	SHIPPING COST:	PROFIT:

Tax DEDUCTIONS

MONTH: _____   **YEAR:** _____

DATE:	DESCRIPTION:	AMOUNT:	NOTES:

Discount TRACKER

MONTH: **YEAR:**

ITEM:	DESCRIPTION:	REG PRICE:	SALE PRICE:

Shipping TRACKER

ORDER #:	PRODUCT DESCRIPTION:	SHIP DATE:	TRACKING #:	SHIPPED:

Supplier CONTACTS

NAME	NAME
BUSINESS	BUSINESS
WEBSITE:	WEBSITE:
EMAIL:	EMAIL:
PHONE:	PHONE:

BUSINESS	BUSINESS
WEBSITE:	WEBSITE:
EMAIL:	EMAIL:
PHONE:	PHONE:

BUSINESS	BUSINESS
WEBSITE:	WEBSITE:
EMAIL:	EMAIL:
PHONE:	PHONE:

BUSINESS	BUSINESS
WEBSITE:	WEBSITE:
EMAIL:	EMAIL:
PHONE:	PHONE:

BUSINESS	BUSINESS
WEBSITE:	WEBSITE:
EMAIL:	EMAIL:
PHONE:	PHONE:

Shipping TRACKER

ORDER NUMBER:	DESCRIPTION OF ITEM:	SHIP DATE:	TRACKING #:

Returns TRACKER

ORDER DATE:	ORDER #:	ITEM DESCRIPTION:	REASON:

 Monthly SALES

JANUARY

FEBRUARY

MARCH

APRIL

MAY

JUNE

Monthly SALES

JULY

AUGUST

SEPTEMBER

OCTOBER

NOVEMBER

DECEMBER

Product PLANNER

PRODUCT DESCRIPTION:

SUPPLIES NEEDED:

PRODUCTION COST BREAKDOWN & EXPENSES

SUPPLIES:

LABOR:

FEES:

STORAGE:

MATERIALS:

SHIPPING:

OTHER:

TOTAL COST:

IMPORTANT NOTES

OTHER INFORMATION

Marketing PLANNER

MONTH: ....

RESOURCES:

START: _____   **END:**

ADVERTISING BREAKDOWN & OVERVIEW

CAMPAIGN: _____   **BUDGET:** _____

AUDIENCE: _____   **COST:** _____

REACH: _____   **LEADS:** _____

TRAFFIC: _____   **REBOOK:** _____

IMPORTANT NOTES

Monthly BUSINESS GOALS

YEAR: ....

JANUARY	FEBRUARY	MARCH

APRIL	MAY	JUNE

JULY	AUGUST	SEPTEMBER

OCTOBER	NOVEMBER	DECEMBER

NOTES:

Yearly BUSINESS GOALS

YEAR:

MAIN OBJECTIVE:

GOAL #1:

GOAL #2:

STEPS I'LL TAKE TO ACHIEVE MY GOALS:

GOAL THIS WILL ACCOMPLISH

Notes

My BUSINESS GOALS

GOAL

START DATE: | DATE OF COMPLETION:

GOAL PROGRESS

GOAL

START DATE: | DATE OF COMPLETION:

GOAL PROGRESS

GOAL

START DATE: | DATE OF COMPLETION:

GOAL PROGRESS

GOAL

START DATE: | DATE OF COMPLETION:

GOAL PROGRESS

GOAL

START DATE: | DATE OF COMPLETION:

GOAL PROGRESS

GOAL

START DATE: | DATE OF COMPLETION::

GOAL PROGRESS

IMPORTANT NOTES | **REMINDERS**

$\mathcal{My}$ BUSINESS GOALS

GOAL

PRIORITY:

🕐 START DATE: DEADLINE:

STEPS TO ACHIEVE MY GOAL:

ACTION STEPS	COMPLETE BY	NOTES

MILESTONES   MILESTONES   MILESTONES

Order FORM

DATE		ORDER #:

CUSTOMER:	EMAIL:	PHONE #:

MAILING ADDRESS:

ITEM#	DESCRIPTION	QTY	PRICE	CUSTOMER NOTES

 # OF PRODUCTS ORDERED:

TOTAL UNIT PRICE: TAX:

APPLIED DISCOUNTS: SHIPPING COST:

PAYMENT METHOD: ORDER DATE:

TOTAL COST:

Order TRACKER

DATE

ORDER #:

CUSTOMER: | **EMAIL:** | **PHONE #:**

PRODUCT:	QTY	SHIP DATE	
			☐
			☐
			☐
			☐
			☐
			☐

PRODUCT:	QTY	SHIP DATE	
			☐
			☐
			☐
			☐
			☐
			☐

TRACKING NUMBER:

DELIVERED

NOTES:

DATE

ORDER #:

CUSTOMER: | **EMAIL:** | **PHONE #:**

PRODUCT:	QTY	SHIP DATE	
			☐
			☐
			☐
			☐
			☐
			☐

PRODUCT:	QTY	SHIP DATE	
			☐
			☐
			☐
			☐
			☐
			☐

TRACKING NUMBER:

DELIVERED

NOTES:

Weekly BUSINESS GOALS

WEEK OF: ....

GOAL:

- [ ]
- [ ]
- [ ]
- [ ]
- [ ]
- [ ]
- [ ]

GOAL:

- [ ]
- [ ]
- [ ]
- [ ]
- [ ]
- [ ]
- [ ]

GOAL:

- [ ]
- [ ]
- [ ]
- [ ]
- [ ]
- [ ]
- [ ]

GOAL:

- [ ]
- [ ]
- [ ]
- [ ]
- [ ]
- [ ]
- [ ]

GOAL:

- [ ]
- [ ]
- [ ]
- [ ]
- [ ]
- [ ]
- [ ]

GOAL:

- [ ]
- [ ]
- [ ]
- [ ]
- [ ]
- [ ]
- [ ]

Business NOTES

Ideas

Notes

Monthly SALES

DATE:	SOURCE	PRICE:	PROFIT:

Monthly INCOME TRACKER

MONTH: _____   **YEAR:** _____

DATE:	DESCRIPTION:	GROSS:	NET:

Monthly EXPENSES

MONTH: **YEAR:**

DATE:	DESCRIPTION:	INVOICE #:	AMOUNT:

Monthly BUDGET

MONTH: _____   **YEAR:** _____

OVERVIEW:	BUDGETED:	ACTUAL COST:
INCOME:		
EXPENSES:		
SAVINGS:		
OTHER:		

EXPENSE TRACKER

SUMMARY:	BUDGETED:	ACTUAL COST:	NOTES:

Product INVENTORY

PRODUCT:	DESCRIPTION:	QTY:	COST:

Mileage TRACKER

PERIOD OF: _____

DATE:	TO:	FROM:	PURPOSE:	TOTAL DISTANCE

Product PRICING

ITEM:	SUPPLY COST:	LABOR:	SHIPPING COST:	PROFIT:

Tax DEDUCTIONS

MONTH: _____ **YEAR:** _____

DATE:	DESCRIPTION:	AMOUNT:	NOTES:

Discount TRACKER

MONTH: **YEAR:**

ITEM:	DESCRIPTION:	REG PRICE:	SALE PRICE:

Shipping TRACKER

ORDER #:	PRODUCT DESCRIPTION:	SHIP DATE:	TRACKING #:	SHIPPED:

Supplier CONTACTS

NAME	NAME
BUSINESS	BUSINESS
WEBSITE:	WEBSITE:
EMAIL:	EMAIL:
PHONE:	PHONE:

BUSINESS	BUSINESS
WEBSITE:	WEBSITE:
EMAIL:	EMAIL:
PHONE:	PHONE:

BUSINESS	BUSINESS
WEBSITE:	WEBSITE:
EMAIL:	EMAIL:
PHONE:	PHONE:

BUSINESS	BUSINESS
WEBSITE:	WEBSITE:
EMAIL:	EMAIL:
PHONE:	PHONE:

BUSINESS	BUSINESS
WEBSITE:	WEBSITE:
EMAIL:	EMAIL:
PHONE:	PHONE:

Shipping TRACKER

ORDER NUMBER:	DESCRIPTION OF ITEM:	SHIP DATE:	TRACKING #:

Returns TRACKER

ORDER DATE:	ORDER #:	ITEM DESCRIPTION:	REASON:

Monthly SALES

JANUARY

FEBRUARY

MARCH

APRIL

MAY

JUNE

Monthly SALES

JULY

AUGUST

SEPTEMBER

OCTOBER

NOVEMBER

DECEMBER

 Product PLANNER

PRODUCT DESCRIPTION:

SUPPLIES NEEDED:

PRODUCTION COST BREAKDOWN & EXPENSES

SUPPLIES:

MATERIALS:

LABOR:

SHIPPING:

FEES:

OTHER:

STORAGE:

TOTAL COST:

IMPORTANT NOTES

OTHER INFORMATION

Marketing PLANNER

MONTH: ....

RESOURCES:

START: _____   **END:** _____

ADVERTISING BREAKDOWN & OVERVIEW

CAMPAIGN: _____

AUDIENCE: _____

REACH: _____

TRAFFIC: _____

BUDGET: _____

COST: _____

LEADS: _____

REBOOK: _____

IMPORTANT NOTES

Monthly BUSINESS GOALS

YEAR: ....

JANUARY	FEBRUARY	MARCH

APRIL	MAY	JUNE

JULY	AUGUST	SEPTEMBER

OCTOBER	NOVEMBER	DECEMBER

NOTES:

Yearly BUSINESS GOALS

YEAR:

MAIN OBJECTIVE:

GOAL #1:	GOAL #2:

STEPS I'LL TAKE TO ACHIEVE MY GOALS:

GOAL THIS WILL ACCOMPLISH

Notes

My BUSINESS GOALS

GOAL

START DATE: DATE OF COMPLETION:

GOAL PROGRESS

GOAL

START DATE: DATE OF COMPLETION:

GOAL PROGRESS

GOAL

START DATE: DATE OF COMPLETION:

GOAL PROGRESS

GOAL

START DATE: DATE OF COMPLETION:

GOAL PROGRESS

GOAL

START DATE: DATE OF COMPLETION:

GOAL PROGRESS

GOAL

START DATE: DATE OF COMPLETION::

GOAL PROGRESS

IMPORTANT NOTES	**REMINDERS**

$\mathcal{My}$ BUSINESS GOALS

GOAL

PRIORITY:

🕐 **START DATE:**   **DEADLINE:**

STEPS TO ACHIEVE MY GOAL:

ACTION STEPS	COMPLETE BY	NOTES

MILESTONES   MILESTONES   MILESTONES

Order FORM

DATE

ORDER #:

CUSTOMER: | EMAIL: | PHONE #:

MAILING ADDRESS:

ITEM#	DESCRIPTION	QTY	PRICE	CUSTOMER NOTES

 # OF PRODUCTS ORDERED:

TOTAL UNIT PRICE: | TAX:

APPLIED DISCOUNTS: | SHIPPING COST:

PAYMENT METHOD: | ORDER DATE:

TOTAL COST:

Order TRACKER

DATE

ORDER #:

CUSTOMER: **EMAIL:**   **PHONE #:**

PRODUCT:	QTY	SHIP DATE		PRODUCT:	QTY	SHIP DATE	
			☐				☐
			☐				☐
			☐				☐
			☐				☐
			☐				☐
			☐				☐

TRACKING NUMBER: **DELIVERED**

NOTES:

DATE

ORDER #:

CUSTOMER: **EMAIL:**   **PHONE #:**

PRODUCT:	QTY	SHIP DATE		PRODUCT:	QTY	SHIP DATE	
			☐				☐
			☐				☐
			☐				☐
			☐				☐
			☐				☐
			☐				☐

TRACKING NUMBER: **DELIVERED**

NOTES:

Weekly BUSINESS GOALS

WEEK OF: ....

GOAL:

- [ ]
- [ ]
- [ ]
- [ ]
- [ ]
- [ ]
- [ ]

GOAL:

- [ ]
- [ ]
- [ ]
- [ ]
- [ ]
- [ ]
- [ ]

GOAL:

- [ ]
- [ ]
- [ ]
- [ ]
- [ ]
- [ ]
- [ ]

GOAL:

- [ ]
- [ ]
- [ ]
- [ ]
- [ ]
- [ ]
- [ ]

GOAL:

- [ ]
- [ ]
- [ ]
- [ ]
- [ ]
- [ ]
- [ ]

GOAL:

- [ ]
- [ ]
- [ ]
- [ ]
- [ ]
- [ ]
- [ ]

Business NOTES

_____
_____
_____
_____
_____
_____
_____
_____
_____
_____
_____
_____
_____
_____
_____
_____
_____

Ideas	*Notes*

Monthly SALES

DATE:	SOURCE	PRICE:	PROFIT:

Monthly INCOME TRACKER

MONTH: **YEAR:**

DATE:	DESCRIPTION:	GROSS:	NET:

Monthly EXPENSES

MONTH: _____ **YEAR:** _____

DATE:	DESCRIPTION:	INVOICE #:	AMOUNT:

Monthly BUDGET

MONTH: **YEAR:**

OVERVIEW:	BUDGETED:	ACTUAL COST:
INCOME:		
EXPENSES:		
SAVINGS:		
OTHER:		

EXPENSE TRACKER

SUMMARY:	BUDGETED:	ACTUAL COST:	NOTES:

Product INVENTORY

PRODUCT:	DESCRIPTION:	QTY:	COST:

Mileage TRACKER

PERIOD OF:

DATE:	TO:	FROM:	PURPOSE:	TOTAL DISTANCE

Product PRICING

ITEM:	SUPPLY COST:	LABOR:	SHIPPING COST:	PROFIT:

Tax DEDUCTIONS

MONTH: **YEAR:**

DATE:	DESCRIPTION:	AMOUNT:	NOTES:

Discount TRACKER

MONTH: _____   **YEAR:** _____

ITEM:	DESCRIPTION:	REG PRICE:	SALE PRICE:

Shipping TRACKER

ORDER #:	PRODUCT DESCRIPTION:	SHIP DATE:	TRACKING #:	SHIPPED:

Supplier CONTACTS

NAME

BUSINESS

WEBSITE:

EMAIL:

PHONE:

NAME

BUSINESS

WEBSITE:

EMAIL:

PHONE:

BUSINESS

WEBSITE:

EMAIL:

PHONE:

BUSINESS

WEBSITE:

EMAIL:

PHONE:

BUSINESS

WEBSITE:

EMAIL:

PHONE:

BUSINESS

WEBSITE:

EMAIL:

PHONE:

BUSINESS

WEBSITE:

EMAIL:

PHONE:

BUSINESS

WEBSITE:

EMAIL:

PHONE:

BUSINESS

WEBSITE:

EMAIL:

PHONE:

BUSINESS

WEBSITE:

EMAIL:

PHONE:

Shipping TRACKER

ORDER NUMBER:	DESCRIPTION OF ITEM:	SHIP DATE:	TRACKING #:

Returns TRACKER

ORDER DATE:	ORDER #:	ITEM DESCRIPTION:	REASON:

Monthly SALES

JANUARY

FEBRUARY

MARCH

APRIL

MAY

JUNE

Monthly SALES

JULY	AUGUST	SEPTEMBER

OCTOBER	NOVEMBER	DECEMBER

Product PLANNER

PRODUCT DESCRIPTION:

SUPPLIES NEEDED:

PRODUCTION COST BREAKDOWN & EXPENSES

SUPPLIES:

MATERIALS:

LABOR:

SHIPPING:

FEES:

OTHER:

STORAGE:

TOTAL COST:

IMPORTANT NOTES

OTHER INFORMATION

Marketing PLANNER

MONTH: ....

RESOURCES:

START: _____   **END:** _____

ADVERTISING BREAKDOWN & OVERVIEW

CAMPAIGN: _____   **BUDGET:** _____

AUDIENCE: _____   **COST:** _____

REACH: _____   **LEADS:** _____

TRAFFIC: _____   **REBOOK:** _____

IMPORTANT NOTES

Monthly BUSINESS GOALS

YEAR: ....

JANUARY	FEBRUARY	MARCH
APRIL	MAY	JUNE
JULY	AUGUST	SEPTEMBER
OCTOBER	NOVEMBER	DECEMBER

NOTES:

Yearly BUSINESS GOALS

YEAR:

GOAL #1:	GOAL #2:

MAIN OBJECTIVE:

STEPS I'LL TAKE TO ACHIEVE MY GOALS:

GOAL THIS WILL ACCOMPLISH

Notes

My BUSINESS GOALS

GOAL

START DATE: DATE OF COMPLETION:

GOAL PROGRESS

GOAL

START DATE: DATE OF COMPLETION:

GOAL PROGRESS

GOAL

START DATE: DATE OF COMPLETION:

GOAL PROGRESS

GOAL

START DATE: DATE OF COMPLETION:

GOAL PROGRESS

GOAL

START DATE: DATE OF COMPLETION:

GOAL PROGRESS

GOAL

START DATE: DATE OF COMPLETION::

GOAL PROGRESS

IMPORTANT NOTES	**REMINDERS**

My BUSINESS GOALS

GOAL

PRIORITY:

START DATE: **DEADLINE:**

STEPS TO ACHIEVE MY GOAL:

ACTION STEPS	COMPLETE BY	NOTES

MILESTONES	MILESTONES	MILESTONES

$Order$ FORM

DATE		ORDER #:

CUSTOMER:	EMAIL:	PHONE #:

MAILING ADDRESS:

ITEM#	DESCRIPTION	QTY	PRICE	CUSTOMER NOTES

OF PRODUCTS ORDERED:

TOTAL UNIT PRICE: TAX:

APPLIED DISCOUNTS: SHIPPING COST:

PAYMENT METHOD: ORDER DATE:

TOTAL COST:

Order TRACKER

DATE		ORDER #:

CUSTOMER:	EMAIL:	PHONE #:

PRODUCT:	QTY	SHIP DATE	
			☐
			☐
			☐
			☐
			☐
			☐

PRODUCT:	QTY	SHIP DATE	
			☐
			☐
			☐
			☐
			☐
			☐

TRACKING NUMBER:	DELIVERED

NOTES:

DATE		ORDER #:

CUSTOMER:	EMAIL:	PHONE #:

PRODUCT:	QTY	SHIP DATE	
			☐
			☐
			☐
			☐
			☐
			☐

PRODUCT:	QTY	SHIP DATE	
			☐
			☐
			☐
			☐
			☐
			☐

TRACKING NUMBER:	DELIVERED

NOTES:

Weekly BUSINESS GOALS

WEEK OF: ....

GOAL:

- [ ] _____
- [ ] _____
- [ ] _____
- [ ] _____
- [ ] _____
- [ ] _____
- [ ] _____

GOAL:

- [ ] _____
- [ ] _____
- [ ] _____
- [ ] _____
- [ ] _____
- [ ] _____
- [ ] _____

GOAL:

- [ ] _____
- [ ] _____
- [ ] _____
- [ ] _____
- [ ] _____
- [ ] _____
- [ ] _____

GOAL:

- [ ] _____
- [ ] _____
- [ ] _____
- [ ] _____
- [ ] _____
- [ ] _____
- [ ] _____

GOAL:

- [ ] _____
- [ ] _____
- [ ] _____
- [ ] _____
- [ ] _____
- [ ] _____
- [ ] _____

GOAL:

- [ ] _____
- [ ] _____
- [ ] _____
- [ ] _____
- [ ] _____
- [ ] _____
- [ ] _____

Business NOTES

Ideas

Notes

Monthly SALES

DATE:	SOURCE	PRICE:	PROFIT:

Monthly INCOME TRACKER

MONTH: _____ **YEAR:** _____

DATE:	DESCRIPTION:	GROSS:	NET:

Monthly EXPENSES

MONTH: **YEAR:**

DATE:	DESCRIPTION:	INVOICE #:	AMOUNT:

Monthly BUDGET

MONTH: _____   **YEAR:** _____

OVERVIEW:	BUDGETED:	ACTUAL COST:
INCOME:		
EXPENSES:		
SAVINGS:		
OTHER:		

EXPENSE TRACKER

SUMMARY:	BUDGETED:	ACTUAL COST:	NOTES:

Product INVENTORY

PRODUCT:	DESCRIPTION:	QTY:	COST:

PERIOD OF: _____

DATE:	TO:	FROM:	PURPOSE:	TOTAL DISTANCE

Product PRICING

ITEM:	SUPPLY COST:	LABOR:	SHIPPING COST:	PROFIT:

Tax DEDUCTIONS

MONTH: _____   **YEAR:** _____

DATE:	DESCRIPTION:	AMOUNT:	NOTES:

Discount TRACKER

MONTH: _____   **YEAR:** _____

ITEM:	DESCRIPTION:	REG PRICE:	SALE PRICE:

Shipping TRACKER

ORDER #:	PRODUCT DESCRIPTION:	SHIP DATE:	TRACKING #:	SHIPPED:

Supplier CONTACTS

NAME ....

BUSINESS ....

WEBSITE: ....

EMAIL: ....

PHONE: ....

NAME ....

BUSINESS ....

WEBSITE: ....

EMAIL: ....

PHONE: ....

BUSINESS ....

WEBSITE: ....

EMAIL: ....

PHONE: ....

BUSINESS ....

WEBSITE: ....

EMAIL: ....

PHONE: ....

BUSINESS ....

WEBSITE: ....

EMAIL: ....

PHONE: ....

BUSINESS ....

WEBSITE: ....

EMAIL: ....

PHONE: ....

BUSINESS ....

WEBSITE: ....

EMAIL: ....

PHONE: ....

BUSINESS ....

WEBSITE: ....

EMAIL: ....

PHONE: ....

BUSINESS ....

WEBSITE: ....

EMAIL: ....

PHONE: ....

BUSINESS ....

WEBSITE: ....

EMAIL: ....

PHONE: ....

Shipping TRACKER

ORDER NUMBER:	DESCRIPTION OF ITEM:	SHIP DATE:	TRACKING #:

Returns TRACKER

ORDER DATE:	ORDER #:	ITEM DESCRIPTION:	REASON:

Monthly SALES

JANUARY

FEBRUARY

MARCH

APRIL

MAY

JUNE

Monthly SALES

JULY	AUGUST	SEPTEMBER

OCTOBER	NOVEMBER	DECEMBER

Product PLANNER

PRODUCT DESCRIPTION:

SUPPLIES NEEDED:

PRODUCTION COST BREAKDOWN & EXPENSES

SUPPLIES:

MATERIALS:

LABOR:

SHIPPING:

FEES:

OTHER:

STORAGE:

TOTAL COST:

IMPORTANT NOTES

OTHER INFORMATION

Marketing PLANNER

MONTH: ....

RESOURCES:

START:

END:

ADVERTISING BREAKDOWN & OVERVIEW

CAMPAIGN:

AUDIENCE:

REACH:

TRAFFIC:

BUDGET:

COST:

LEADS:

REBOOK:

IMPORTANT NOTES

Monthly BUSINESS GOALS

YEAR: ....

JANUARY	FEBRUARY	MARCH

APRIL	MAY	JUNE

JULY	AUGUST	SEPTEMBER

OCTOBER	NOVEMBER	DECEMBER

NOTES:

Yearly BUSINESS GOALS

YEAR:

GOAL #1:	GOAL #2:

MAIN OBJECTIVE:

STEPS I'LL TAKE TO ACHIEVE MY GOALS:

GOAL THIS WILL ACCOMPLISH

Notes

My BUSINESS GOALS

GOAL

START DATE: DATE OF COMPLETION:

GOAL PROGRESS

GOAL

START DATE: DATE OF COMPLETION:

GOAL PROGRESS

GOAL

START DATE: DATE OF COMPLETION:

GOAL PROGRESS

GOAL

START DATE: DATE OF COMPLETION:

GOAL PROGRESS

GOAL

START DATE: DATE OF COMPLETION:

GOAL PROGRESS

GOAL

START DATE: DATE OF COMPLETION::

GOAL PROGRESS

IMPORTANT NOTES	**REMINDERS**

My BUSINESS GOALS

GOAL

PRIORITY:

🕐 START DATE: DEADLINE:

STEPS TO ACHIEVE MY GOAL:

ACTION STEPS	COMPLETE BY	NOTES

MILESTONES   MILESTONES   MILESTONES

70779465R00084

Made in the USA
Middletown, DE
28 September 2019